The author, illustrator and editor would like to thank
Jim Hayward of the Carterton Breeding Aviaries for
his advice on parrots.

Kingfisher Books, Grisewood & Dempsey Ltd,
Elsley House, 24–30 Great Titchfield Street,
London W1P 7AD

First published in paperback in 1992 by Kingfisher Books
10 9 8 7 6 5 4 3 2 1
Originally published in hardback in 1989 by Kingfisher Books

BRITISH CATALOGUING IN PUBLICATION DATA
A catalogue record for this book is
available from the British Library

ISBN 0 86272 525 9

Edited by Camilla Hallinan
Designed by Ben White
Cover design by Pinpoint Design Company
Phototypeset by Southern Positives and
Negatives (SPAN), Lingfield, Surrey
Colour separations by Scantrans Pte Ltd, Singapore
Printed in Spain

MICHAEL CHINERY

ALL
ABOUT
BABY
ANIMALS

Illustrated by
Ian Jackson

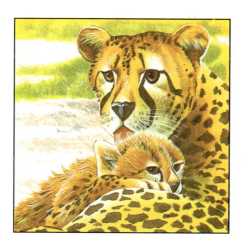

Kingfisher Books

Contents

All around

Baby animals live in all kinds of places, on land and in the water.

Snails lay their eggs on the ground and among rotting leaves where their babies can find plenty to eat.

Baby woodpeckers grow up in tree holes which their parents make with their sharp beaks.

These prairie marmots are leaving the burrow where they were born. The adults watch over them and bark warnings if they spot any danger.

Rocky Mountain goats live high in the mountains. Their kids can climb well even when they are only a few hours old.

Moorhens build their nests on ponds and streams. Their chicks tumble into the water and swim as soon as they hatch.

The baby dolphin is born in the sea. Its mother nudges it to the surface so that it can take its first breath.

Getting ready

Before they have their babies, many animals make safe homes for them. Sometimes the mother makes the nest, sometimes the father, and sometimes both parents share the work.

The mother polar bear digs a den deep in a snow drift. Her cubs are born there in the winter. Away from the cold wind, the den stays warm and snug.

Female tailor birds make cosy nests by sewing leaves together with hair and spider silk. They use their beaks as needles.

White storks build huge untidy nests with sticks. They often build on houses.

The female potter wasp makes her nest with clay. She lays an egg inside and covers it with food. Then she closes the nest and never goes back to it.

The mother rabbit prepares a nursery burrow for her babies. She lines it with soft grass and with her own fur.

Birth

Many animals lay eggs. Each egg contains a growing baby and a supply of food.

Other babies feed and grow inside their mothers' bodies until they are ready to be born.

Birds hatch from eggs. The babies break the shells with their beaks. Ostriches are the biggest birds of all, and their eggs each weigh about 1.5 kilogrammes.

Most reptiles, fish and insects hatch from eggs. This baby snake is a reptile.

Animal numbers

Animals have families of different sizes. Some give birth to one or two babies at a time, once a year. Others have more babies, more often. Many of the animals that lay eggs have lots of babies.

One
panda cub

Two
deer fawns

This zebra has just given birth to her foal, which has been growing inside her body for a year.

Some baby animals spend two years inside their mothers' bodies, others are born after a few weeks.

Five
hedgehog young

Ten
blue tit chicks

Hundreds of
frog tadpoles

Weak and strong

Some babies are completely helpless when they are born. Their parents look after them until they are big and strong. Other babies are up and about soon after birth.

Hares are born with fur and with their eyes open. They are born above ground and can run through the grass when only a few minutes old.

Rabbits are blind and naked when they are born. Their mother cares for them in the safety of the burrow. They go out after about three weeks.

Geese and many other birds that nest on the ground can run and swim as soon as they hatch, but their parents show them how to find food.

Many birds are helpless when they hatch and do not even have feathers. Swifts are fed and kept warm by their parents for several weeks in the nest.

Giraffes wander over the plains in herds and give birth to their babies in the open. If the young do not keep up with the herd they are killed and eaten by other animals.

This giraffe is helping her newborn calf to stand up. It will be able to walk within an hour and will stay close to its mother.

Parents

Sometimes both the mother and the father look after their babies. They may share all the work or they may do different jobs. Sometimes only one parent looks after the babies.

Golden eagle parents both help to rear their babies. The father brings the food, which the mother tears up and feeds to them. When the eaglets are larger and need more food both parents go out to hunt.

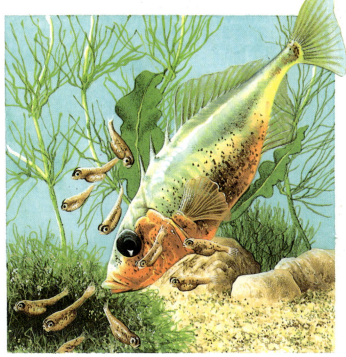

Emperor penguins take it in turn to hold their chick on their feet and keep it warm and off the ice.

The male stickleback is in charge of the babies. He chases them back if they swim too far from the nest.

Baby mammals, the furry animals, stay with their mother because at first they need milk from her body.

These young cheetahs will stay with their mother for over a year while they learn to hunt for food.

All alone

Many animals abandon their eggs as soon as they have laid them and never see their babies. The babies have to find their own food and look after themselves right from the start.

The swallowtail butterfly leaves her eggs, but she makes sure that she lays them on the right plants for her babies.

The baby butterfly is a caterpillar. When it hatches from its egg it eats the leaves which its mother chose for it.

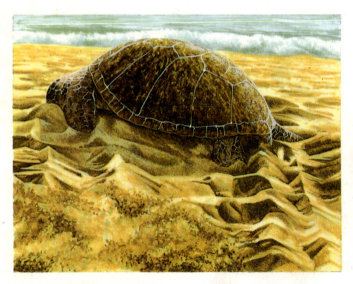

Sea turtles come ashore to lay their eggs. They bury them in the sand and then waddle back into the water.

Baby turtles have to make their own way to the sea. Many are eaten by birds before they get there.

Cuckoos fly away after laying their eggs in other birds' nests. The new parents look after the babies.

They have to work hard because cuckoos babies are big and need plenty of food.

Carrying the baby

Instead of building nests, some animals use their own bodies as nurseries for their babies. Usually it is the mother that carries the babies, until they can look after themselves.

The baby kangaroo is called a joey. It stays in its mother's pouch for eight months. Even after that it hops back for a rest.

The Surinam toad carries her babies in tiny pouches on her back. Each pouch is like a pond, with one tadpole which turns into a little toad and jumps out.

The baby koala goes everywhere with its mother. It spends six months in her pouch and another six months clinging to her back.

This mouth-brooding fish carries its eggs and babies in its mouth. The babies go out to explore but dash back if they are frightened.

Baby scorpions ride on their mother's back. They jump off after a few days and begin to hunt for their first meals.

Feeding-time

Many animals can find food for themselves as soon as they are born. Others need help from their parents.

This baby pelican is searching for fish in its mother's throat. The chicks can catch fish for themselves when they are ten weeks old.

Most spiderlings get no help from their parents, but this comb-footed spider bites flies so that her babies can drink the juices that trickle out.

Baby mammals all drink milk from their mothers' bodies at first. They are gradually weaned off milk as they learn to eat other food.

A mouse can have six or seven babies. She feeds them all with milk, but only for about 18 days.

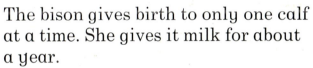

The bison gives birth to only one calf at a time. She gives it milk for about a year.

This baby rhinoceros started to graze with its mother when it was only a week old, but it goes on drinking her milk for about a year.

Bear grows up

Brown bears are born in the winter. The newborn cubs are about 20 centimetres long and weigh only 500 grammes. They have hardly any hair. Their mother looks after them all by herself, keeping them warm and feeding them with milk.

The cubs leave the den when they are about two months old. They are still very small and their mother often carries them in her mouth.

The cubs play together in the summer and discover all sorts of new things to eat. They grow big and strong and soon weigh 20 kilogrammes.

The cubs stay with their mother until they are at least a year old. They learn how to hunt by watching her. Soon they will be able to catch fish themselves.

Joining the family

Some baby animals are part of a large family group.
Baboon families are called troupes and there may be
more than 50 animals in one troupe. A new baby
spends its first month in its mother's arms and the
other baboons come to stroke it. Then the baby rides
around on its mother's back.

When it is about three months old it starts to play with the other baboons. By playing with each other the young baboons soon learn which are strong and which are weak. The weak ones learn not to argue with the strong ones, so they all live together in peace.

Playtime

Baby mammals spend a lot of time playing. Chasing and wrestling each other helps their muscles to grow properly and keeps them fit and alert. It's fun too.

Elephants love to play in the water. The babies have tussles and squirt water everywhere with their trunks. If they squirt an adult they get a smack to teach them how to behave properly as they grow up in the herd. The females help each other to look after the calves.

Fox cubs learn about hunting by chasing each other. Chasing leaves and feathers teaches them how to pounce on mice and other small animals when they have to catch their own food.

Otter cubs like nothing better than sliding down muddy banks into the water. They soon become strong swimmers. The adults are playful too. They seem to enjoy playing just for the fun of it.

Keeping clean

Animals spend a lot of time washing and grooming their babies. Cleaning them keeps them healthy and makes them more comfortable.

A lioness cleans her cub with her large rough tongue. The cubs will groom each other as they get older. Adult males are not very interested in washing, so their manes are often rather dirty.

Few insects look after their babies. But the female earwig is always licking her eggs and babies to keep them clean and free from germs.

This flamingo chick is having its feathers preened by its mother. Clean and tidy coats help birds to stay warm and dry.

The blue jay takes away its babies' droppings regularly. Otherwise the nest would become dirty and smelly and the chicks might become ill.

Parrot grows up

These parrots nest in tree holes. They usually lay just two eggs. The mother sits on the eggs for about a month, and then the eggs hatch. The baby parrots are blind and naked and quite helpless.

When they are hungry they squeal like puppies, until the mother gives them fruit and seeds and other food collected by the father.

The chicks' skin gets darker after a few days and grows grey fluffy down.

The first proper feathers start to appear when the chicks are about four weeks old. This is when they begin to get their bright colours. The males become green and the females become red.

When they are about three months old the chicks clamber out of the nest. They start looking for food, although their parents still feed them. The chicks flap their wings and make their first short flights. They are a little unsteady at first, but they are soon strong enough to fly away.

It will be a year or more before the parrots get their rich adult colours. When they are about three years old they will have nests and eggs of their own.

Baby talk

Baby animals have different ways of telling their parents that they are lost or cold or hungry.

When hungry chicks open their beaks their bright yellow throats tell the parents to put food in. These are little wrens.

The seagull chick taps the red spot on its parent's beak to say that it is hungry.

Many animals recognize each other by their different smell. This seal always knows her own pup by its smell. They sniff "hello".

This young spider monkey is lost but its parents will soon hear its loud cries and come to rescue it.

Spider monkeys are noisy creatures. The parents bark like dogs to warn their babies of danger.

Protecting the baby

Baby animals need to be kept safe from danger.
Their parents protect them in many ways.

This hippopotamus has seen a crocodile looking for
food. She gets between it and her baby. The crocodile
will not risk attacking the calf now.

Babies must be kept warm. These
young snowy owls are very snug
under their mother's feathers.

The male swan protects his cygnets
by flapping his powerful wings and
hissing loudly at intruders.

The crocodile carries her babies from the nursery where they hatch to the safety of the river. No harm will come to the babies between her teeth.

This plover fools the fox by fluttering along the ground as if it had a broken wing. The fox follows the bird and does not see the chicks. When far away from its nest the bird flies off.

Salmon grows up

The salmon lays thousands of eggs in the autumn, in a hole which she digs in the gravel on the river bed. She covers her eggs with gravel and then swims away.

Salmon babies are about two centimetres long when they hatch in the spring. They are called fry, and each one has a food-filled yolk sac.

For six weeks the baby salmon lives on the food in its yolk sac. The sac shrinks as the food is used up. Then the fish starts to eat microscopic animals.

When the yolk sac has gone the young salmon is called a parr. It gets black spots on its sides and grows to about 15 centimetres long.

At about two years of age the salmon becomes silvery and is called a smolt. It swims down the river to the sea and feeds there for a year or two.

When the salmon is three or four years old it goes back to the river where it grew up. It may be a metre long and it is a strong swimmer. It can even leap over waterfalls on its way up to the breeding grounds. But the long journey is tiring and many salmon die after laying their eggs.

Whose baby?

Some baby animals do not look at all like their parents. They change shape as they grow up and some change their homes and habits too.

This microscopic baby will turn into a crab.

This baby fish will flatten out to become a plaice.

Wriggly tadpoles grow up into frogs.

This grub will change into a beautiful ladybird.

These mosquito larvae will grow wings and leave the water.

Crab

Plaice

Frog

Ladybird

Mosquito

41

Tiger moth grows up

Moths and butterflies are insects that start life as eggs. The larvae that hatch do not look anything like their parents and are called caterpillars.

1 Tiger moth caterpillars bite their way out of the eggs in the summer and start to nibble the leaves. They grow slowly, and after a few weeks they hide away and go to sleep for the winter. Not all caterpillars sleep through the winter.

2 When it wakes up in the spring, the caterpillar starts to eat again. It grows quickly, so its skin gets tight. It wriggles out of its skin and grows a new, looser one. This happens several times in a caterpillar's lifetime.

3 By June the caterpillar is fully grown and it spins a silken cocoon around itself. It turns into a chrysalis inside this shelter.

6 When its wings have hardened the moth is ready to fly. It will find a mate and produce babies of its own.

Birth, growing up and having a family are all part of an animal's life cycle.

5 The new moth climbs a plant and then sits still while its wings swell to full size. They are soft at first but they soon harden.

4 Inside the chrysalis an adult moth is forming. After a few weeks the moth struggles out. Its wings are small and crumpled.

Baby names

Many animals have special names for their babies. Perhaps you know some of them.

Baby dogs are called **pups.** So are baby seals.

Cats have **kittens.** So do rabbits.

Calves are baby cows and baby elephants.

There are lots of other names for baby animals. You can find the ones below in this book.

calves bison dolphins elephants giraffes hippos rhinos	**chicks** most birds **cubs** brown bears cheetahs foxes lions	**cygnets** swans **eaglets** eagles **fawns** deer	**fry** all fish **goslings** geese **grubs** ladybirds	**kids** goats **kittens** rabbits **larvae** many insects	**owlets** owls **pups** seals **spiderlings** spiders
caterpillars butterflies moths	otters pandas polar bears	**foals** zebras	**joeys** kangaroos	**leverets** hares	**tadpoles** frogs toads

Index